More on Infrared...

Infrared is a luminous book! Janet Trenchard paints with words, as in her opening poem, Spirits: "I need the color amber in the palm of my hand..." Words emerge "as trumpets summoned up/from underground that dark gold/that everything is made of, ..." Poems of smoke, night owls, scarab beetles, or a weekend at God's, are painted with an imagistic brush. Here, too, is an old Wedgewood stove lighting a table that holds, like Janet's poems, a book filled with whale posters, a clawfoot tub, Nina Simone on the stereo. One is drawn in, as in her final lines, "angels in the Torah bending over/each blade of grass..."

Dane Cervine, author of *How Therapists Dance* and *The Jeweled Net of Indra*.

Infrared

by

Janet
Trenchard

Infrared written by:
Janet Trenchard all rights reserved

Library of Congress #: 2016938468

ISBN #: 978-0-9778645-7-7

Publisher:

Blue Bone Books
P.O. Box 2250
Santa Cruz, CA 95063

Cover Art and all insets by Janet Trenchard

Book designer and editor:
Robin Lysne, Ph.D. with Janet Trenchard

Blue Bone Books is a cooperative poetry press, and also publishes children's, and metaphysical books. Formed in 2007, the press formed its cooperative poetry collective in 2013.

Acknowledgements

A huge thanks to:
    The Blue Bone Poets,
    The Emerald Street Poets,
    especially Joanna Martin.

Special thanks to Seena Frost,
    creator of the amazing
    SoulCollage process.

For Adrian and Kevin

Infrared
Table of Contents

Dark Gold — 8

Spirits	10
Dark Gold	11
Smoke	12
Night Owls	13
Jazz Jam	14
Bang it, Baby	15
Time to Glitter	16
Weekend at God's	18
Mothers, Gods, and Angels	21
Moon of Shortest Nights	22
What Falls Through	23

Time and Weather — 24

The Silence of Books	26
Dream #3	27
Renunciate	28
Salt Shaker	29
Talking Salamanders	30
Scarab	31
Circling	32
Thread	33
Bad Weather	34
Old Houses	35
Bail Out, 2008	36
What Women Are Wearing	37
Psychometry	38
Phone Messages	39

Smithereens — 40

Hatchings	42
Head First	44
Interstate 580	45
Antlers	46
The Two Things	47
Insomnia	48
Pie Shakti	49
Vanishing Point	50
Cool Side	51
Evening Waters	52
Stairway	53
It Parts Like Water	54
Galapagos	55
Burnt Offerings	56

Infrared — 58

Infrared	60
Jackson Street	61
Valerian	62
Wine Coolers	63
Offering	64
Wisdom of Hands	65
Journey	66
The Gifts	67
Wedgewood Stove	68
Lifeline	69
Sparks	70
Diamond Pattern	71
Vintage	72
Prickly Pear	73
Logos	74
Author Biography	76

Previously Published Poems

"Bang it, Baby", "Infrared", "Antlers" (under the name, "Strange Wind") and "Interstate 580", and "Hatchings" have all been published in Porter Gulch Review under either Janet Crawford or Janet Trenchard.

"Scarab" has been published in Caesura, The Journal of Poetry Center San Jose. "Spirits", "Mothers, Gods, and Angels," have been published in Diamond Dust, and "Moon of Shortest Nights" received Honorable Mention in the Los Gatos Poetry Contest.

Dark Gold

Spirits

I need the color amber
in the palm of my hand,
to swirl it
and gaze at it
through the glass,
to feel its warmth spread
through my chest.
Not this transparent spirit
vacuous as the echo
of a swinging door,
a lone olive eyeballing me
from the depths.
Around me, voices,
walking footprints,
not much else.

Dark Gold

Last night a door opened
onto a smoky stage
and I entered, trembling.
Men pranced and strutted,
their faces surrendered to spirits
as trumpets summoned up
from underground that dark gold
that everything is made of.
I drank the molten gold
pouring forth in warm shafts
sweet and dense as honey,
my arms moving
like snakes.

Smoke

Shooting in the dark
she turns over stones
searching for blueprints
a key, a code

she turns over stones
shaking her pan for words
a code, a key
something made of gold

shakes her pan of words
rough, smooth or sharp
for something made of gold
or at least not made of smoke

rough, smooth or sharp
she'll take anything
not made of smoke
though most words are

she'll take anything
to be an encoded truth
and most words are, at best
a shot in the dark.

Night Owls

My friend, the owl expert
and I drank our way
through happy hour
and into the evening
as she explained that certain owls
could sound like a woman crying,
or a whispered "hush", loud and long,
some owls seemed to cry "whisssskey",
others make sounds
like the men at the next table,
soft, rhythmic, punctuated
with low explosive tones,
the keening of a flute,
the deep low sigh of bass viol.
For me, it was enough to know
that it could be owls
calling to me through whiskey,
hooting through Delta blues,
and whispering through the men
at the next table.

Jazz Jam

Each player wobbles
his own sad sonata
like a planet on its axis
before being called back
into orbit by a wail
centuries old
rising in the throat
like a phosphorescent tide
illuminating neckbones
while blue smoke rings
float through space
like asteroid belts
set loose

Bang it, Baby

Better blow some life
into those eyes,
sweetheart, go down
and get a drink at the All Faiths Bar,
where your friend, Preacher,
looks you in the face
all the way through,and says softly,
Can you get yourself together?
and you wonder as you back away,
and you don't know if you should get a tattoo
or a turban, or maybe just a bourbon,
you're teetering on the edge, a barstool away
from salvation, when out the window
you see a gang of misfits, and mystics,
troublemakers and troubadors.
Someone hands you a tambourine.

Time to Glitter

On the balcony, the girl in yellow chiffon
holds a martini delicately
against the sunset,
hair like Alice in Wonderland
she hasn't gone down the rabbit hole yet,
but the pendulum swings,
there are martinis in the lower realms too
where they gulp at beauty like vampires,
and when you follow them down
in satin pumps, you swear
you'll remember the way back.
The hostess in her apron,
spinner of worlds
from sugar, eggs, and whatever's handy,
welcomes the new guy standing
at the door in a suit and tie.
So young. So handsome.
Everyone turns to him, smiling
in a dreamy dance as he leads them
out into the night to look at the stars.
One by one, he points them out
giving them different names
than the ones you know,
and as the party slowly fades into dawn

you understand that it's only
a matter of time before
you'll wake up and be given
new names too.

Weekend at God's

There we were as the sun came up
standing around on the lawn
in dress shoes
we'd partied all night.

Passing the kitchen I heard God's wife
complain as she tried to wrestle
something out of the freezer
*We've bar-b-cued almost everything
in creation.*

I looked around me,
God's place out in the country
was well--palatial--and I
was struck with the feeling
I'd been here before
there out in back
behind those olive trees,
someone used to live there,
someone I had to see.

No one noticed me
slip away behind the trees
where I spotted the little shack

just as it was before.
I passed some dark skinned men
working on the grounds
they said, *yes, it's her*
she's still there
o most definitely.

Her hut was flimsy
and smaller than I remembered,
God's mother isn't at all like
what we think,
she's incredibly fat
for one thing.

I looked in,
stringy black hair
hung round her neck,
long pendulous breasts
reached toward the ground,
she was enormous.

She didn't apologize like last time
(last time we had to peel the caked earth
off her).

She's busy, she runs a little business
out of her hut called
BOOKS FROM THE CENTER OF THE EARTH.
The sky was dark with clouds,
I had to get back.
She gave me a book,
she said keep it.

Heading back to the party
I opened it,
thunder rolled,
drops of water hit the page,
mud oozed up from the binding
and as I reached the lawn
everyone was standing
heels deep in it
looking dazed,
soggy paper cups
and cigarettes
still in their hands.

Mothers, Gods, and Angels

Reminding us of the ring
of fine crystal, continuously heard
in the backgound of everything,
they sit, as in ancient times,
in togas, aprons, or silk pajamas,
sipping and tasting,
touching and sensing,
selecting for the table
that's always before us,
sometimes seen only through smoke,
sometimes seen only through tears,
heard through the noise of the street,
heard through the noise of the mind,
we close our eyes,
raise our glasses
to them.

Moon of Shortest Nights

Moon of shortest nights floating
over the secret Sanskrit
that only you can write with your light
and through the netting,
which in these last months
lies over the vineyard, that netting
that only you can pass through,
pass through, moon of shortest nights,
leave traces of your soft light on the grapes,
to pass through into heavy bottles
that will lie huddled in the basement
all through the long winter
and the coming years
then pass your secret light
through the dark pour
into the glass.

What Falls Through

Day falls through night,
a shooting star,
night falls into day,
raven on a wire,
yesterday falls into tomorrow
humming an old tune,
dusk falls through bougainvillea
dressed in lace.
Through eyes, cupped hands,
and words, we fall,
stones in the stream,
smoothed and turned,
rounded, by what falls through.

Time and Weather

The Silence Of Books

Worn pages, eroded as if by wind, dust,
gently ripped away in large sections
like facades of demolished buildings
in an old newsreel, silent
like angry hieroglyphs of twisted rebar,
silent like blown out candles,
silent like an ancient city
whispering its love cry
from just under
the blowing sand.

Dream #3

Barefoot, I walk the railroad track
in a nectar-colored gown
searching for the city of purple palms
pools that quiver in the dark
like electric aqua jellyfish
twentyfive tables on a grassy knoll
the garden party of the gods
where blackeyed men in velvet vests
play "Perfidia" in the shade
of the cypress trees that surround
the Spanish mansion where
my dead grandmother
now lives.

Renunciate

Night after night I slip away from this convent,
cross a shallow river barefoot to roam
the overgrown orchard of my ancestral lands.
I move swiftly among dark trees,
fingers tracing rough bark,
face slapped by tiny branches
I have only so much time.
before the first rays of dawn I hurry back
cross again the shallow river
sink my arms down in its stone cold waters
claw the sandy bottom, searching
for what was mine, lost,
discarded, renounced, denied,
on my knees, pleading with God,
Give it back!

Salt Shaker

Right now as the rain starts to fall
I feel my lifeforce bleed gently into it.
Things slip out of my grasp,
my tenacity is set loose.
The loneliness of a salt shaker
rings out in silence
onto the emptiness of a formica counter,
dim light from the window
washing over it,
shadows of the day.
Salt, giver of structure to all living things
and the sharp taste of truth
on the tongue.

Talking Salamanders

If my toenails bore
the chipped remains of frosty orange,
pink or red, I could almost see
the thin, milky line
that silhouettes the skin
of the Disney heroine like electricity
begin to trace my toes and fingers
with that glow...
but was it only on their skin?
Setting them apart?
Denoting a magical race
self-luminous, radiant,
put here to be our gods?
Or did they simply inhabit
an atavistic realm,
Latterday Animists
talking to salamanders,
the holy grace shining out of everything?

*Some years ago a document appeared within the Mormon archives revealing that the angel who appeared to Joseph Smith was really a salamander. Wondrous! Sadly this was declared a "hoax" by church authorities.

Scarab

The scarab beetle
crawls across the sky
pushing that fertile bundle of eggs
that ball of dung

Crawling across the sky
recreating the world daily
by rolling a ball of dung
turning a page each day

Recreating the world daily
days stack up against each other
like pages of books by the ancient gnostics
those heretics, and other theologians

Pitted against each other
crawling across the sky
the ancient gnostics and other theologians
push their bundles like beetles.

Circling

Life, I want to get caught
in your web
drink your sticky nectar
eat evil food off your buffet
swoon like jello
into your liquid body
swim blindly
perhaps after centuries
to float up through some window
into a chamber
of shadow light
where two whispering mouths
move continuously
and what soundless waterfall
tumbles from those lips?
It's nothing new
only Life, once again
the whole parade.

Thread

With a quick leap backward in time,
following her thread, she slips through
a clerestory window here,
a crenelated arch there,
but when bricks and columns begin to crumble,
she scurries under a bridge, round the corner,
down a cobblestone street,
for though the structures ring with voices,
the cries of animals,
the scent of smoke,
in the end they are not much more than dust.
Laughing, she looks up,
her hat in her hands,
a light rain begins to fall.

Bad Weather

According to some
she finally returned
sweaty hair and a jacket
that had seen some bad weather

She finally returned
with the appearance of one
who had seen bad weather
and survived on olives

with the appearance of one
who has been through a wormhole
surviving on olives
and slices of lemon

a wormhole on ice
with slices of lemon
no one can say
she had nothing to eat

sweaty hair and a jacket
that reeked of gin
she never returned
according to some.

Old Houses

This hillside stacked with houses
chalky white, the white of powder
spiderwebs, fog, and the smoke
from peoples' mouths.

Cracked and broken windows,
long and narrow, allow wind
in and out of darkened rooms
carrying secrets like a scent.

As a child I feared wolves I'd never seen,
or talking wolves, the ones in books.
White paint chipping off bedposts
didn't bother me.

Now old houses follow me,
sucking at my bones,
they call to me in papery whispers:
This is your door, come on in
here is your bed, your ragged quilt,
your broken dishes...
I take a deep breath
and walk on.

Bailout, 2008

A Babylonian goddess pointed at me
and money, jobs, and houses
flew up in the air over Kansas
and suddenly I was a stripper
in a dress made of dollars,
peeling off a dollar to each beat of the drum,
until, in the finale, naked,
arms out to each side,
chin up, I cried,
'Bring me my wings!
I have immortal longings in me!'

What Women Are Wearing

Adorn yourself with bones and feathers
    animal prints are back. Wear cheetah
and move like one on the runway
    choose accessories
but don't be one, avoid glass,
but stay clear, travel light
    move at night
the phone call from antiquity
    comes quickly
        and unexpectedly.

Psychometry

She wears a headdress
with a bird facing backwards,
touches a pillar, a chunk of cement,
her fingers read the objects
as scenes rush before her eyes,
the power of reading the past;

After our visit with the psychometrist
we were ready.
We found Lot's wife and joined arms,
set off across the desert,
one of us waving a middle finger.

Phone Messages

This caller won't give up!
She leaves a desperate message that says,
Bring me my wings,
I have immortal longings in me!

This call comes from deep within.
A raspy whisper says:
I am your unspoken rage.
Call me.

This one is a young girl calling from the ruins.
She's been walking for days
over plywood and old mattresses.
She says the debris has finally begun to thin out,
you can see patches of bare earth again.
A pomegranate in one hand
and a cell phone in the other,
she wants to know
how to reset the code.

SMITHEREENS

Hatchings

Once I woke up inside
a sandstorm
and crawled out on my belly.
I stood up and saw
with the eyes of a god
and breathed the pure air,
that rung with my laughter.

Years later,
driving home from the store,
I wake up again
as if from a dream
to find myself in a driveway
among a wilderness of rooftops.

Like a baby bird cracking its shell,
I open the car door,
step out,
look around in wonder,
the key in my hand,

an X that says
you are here
on a map
of the moon.

Head First

Head first and with the grace of spiders
the underbody
suddenly visible this morning
in shiny wet pavement
dropping down like a plumbline
as if, having declined from the start
to live above ground
had simply turned and dived down
into vastness
to drink at some reservoir
of black space
sucking it up through long
strawlike legs, rootlike, arterial
up through the rainslick asphalt
into the hollows of my bones.

Interstate 580
For Jeff

The moon sprays platinum
among dark trees,
the glow of payless drugs
floats by so lightly,
intimate and unknown,
an icon of our world,
like headlights carried on arms
of warm dark air,
ghostly machine guns
blowing us to smithereens.

Antlers

It's a strange wind blowing up this street
the windows are odd shapes
reflecting everything, revealing nothing,
antlers nailed to a doorway
point to eternal things.
The agents of entropy are all around us,
they come to us thirsty and hungry
in our time of trouble.
If I could just bake them a cake of my darkness
fill chipped china cups
with the wine of our regret
they would eat this food for us
as only they know how to do.

The Two Things

It's almost midnight
and I think of Norm
out on some deserted highway
driving around in his patrol car
staring at the lights of the valley
keeping his eye on the moon
it jumps out at you when you least expect it
when you're so confused you don't
even know where it is
and the two things
that have been on his mind for days
the song he's been humming
flip, flop fly, I don't care if I die
and what the bank robber told him;
there's nothing so quiet
as the inside
of a vault.

Insomnia

Empty beer and wine bottles
ghosts of the small hours huddle
dreamy skeletons
on top of the refrigerator
tulip lampshade
supposed to be cute
glad there was someone who saw to cute
when they had the chance
someone selected it
had it installed
proving that even cute once had its day
in the night kitchen
luxury in a linoleum desert
a tiny irony
a grace.

Pie Shakti

He had passed through blue doorways
in a suit and tie
gained entrance into temples and
white cloud pavilions,
wandered among lost
lords of the underworld
with their cigars and raybans
their beards and motorcycles,
they forgave him,
they seemed to take
his sins upon themselves
with a wink,
and a clink of glasses.

All his searching and yet
he had overlooked her.
How had he missed this point of light,
barefeet planted in American dirt,
Jesus written all over her face?
He opened himself to the touch
of her radiant squash-blessing,
thunderclouds gathered,
natural laws were broken.
His heart opened
like a pumpkin in the rain.

Vanishing Point

Under a roof of leaves
A cat and I walk slowly up a street
from opposite sides
toward some center where it seems
that everything must meet:
the street, a hill drowned in oak shade
the cat, black as Robert Alvarado's hair
and me, a girl who could fall forever
staring into it.

Cool Side

Exhausted by relentless radiance,
the sun, self-eclipsed, stepped out
through the burning hole as a moon
into a rice paper sky,
skim milk on a glass plate.
No one knew the sun
had a cool introspective side,
and dreamed of hanging out
at a seaside bar
wrapped in white chiffon.

Evening Waters

Across rippled waters
clouds stretch like dusky wings
against a persimmon sky
small lights strung carelessly
over a few black posts
a ruined pier.
Like sailors at night
we fasten our gaze on these twinkling lights
as they appear and disappear
stitching dark waves to the glowing sky.
Like undersea creatures that morph
to match their surroundings,
small lights beckon,
quickening something in me
like the doctrine of signatures
joining like unto like
in a vast darkening sky.

Stairway

Even here in the hills
where it seems there is nothing
in the world but stars
and oaks, there is
a manhole cover
fitted flat to its pavement home,
a perfect disc in the moonlight,
rounding to fullness
as I come near.

yet in the dark it appears to float,
glowing, naked of gravity,
a stairway to the moon
-itself a stairway
to the sun-
humbled now, fallen,
a moon of the streets,
it whispers
"walk on me"
as I pass by.

It Parts Like Water

First thing this morning
walking out into it
arms and thighs are suspended
in soft thick light

I walk out into
a reversed architecture
of light and shadow
-a fly in amber

In reverse architecture
I'm a negative
a fly in amber, caught
for a split second

A negative shape
that light parts around
for a split second
around and past

It parts like water
parting for a boat
around and past me
like the morning.

Galapagos

For thousands of years
I've wandered this desert
whose vastness stretches
longer than the equator.
I've wandered until my body
was an empty flask
of handblown glass,
blown and spun
from heat and wind,
when suddenly,
I pass into a new geography,
gasping, a creature thrown
upon the banks of a new world,
ravished by its opulent sadness,
cheeks flushed, heart moist
and fleshy like a swollen tongue,
hungry, to taste at last
it's rightful food.

Burnt Offerings

Barbara in the doorway,
her wild hair gray now, pulled back,
no pearls, no makeup her thick hands
could be patting flatbread
over a stone oven
out on some rocky desert
beneath a vengeful sky.

In the yard, desks sit on couches
flanked by dressers,
lamps, chairs, a makeshift altar
to a demanding god,
one that would crunch
glass coffee tables
like ice cubes.

I wander in awe from room
to gutted room, carpets stripped,
concrete floors a solid ground
for her work.

The slate entryway where
the giant treefern once stood, skylit,
opens onto large rooms
inhabited now by her sculptures,
as graceful as natural stone formations
in some underground cavern
or on the moon.

In the doorway between past and present,
husbands and children all grown up and gone,
no margarita, no furniture, no apology,
just the huge white forms,
their backlit silhouettes
rising and falling from room
to darkening room, like the ocean,
like smoke.

INFRARED

Infrared

I keep a jug of red wine
in the bushes for night walks,
fill my coffee mug,
cupping it like ruby fire,
because the light
is draining out of everything.

The wind hisses but I hear
only the echoes of curses,
pops and whistles
spinning themselves out
like pinwheeling firecrackers.

I drink red wine as the long
black tongue of pavement
slowly swallows the light.
A cool moon rises, a squid in ink.

I wrap myself in my shawl
to hold in my warmth,
I'm infrared,
a mouse on the desert at night.

Jackson Street

This morning you wake me
on the telephone.
It takes me back to Jackson Street,
sunshine slamming down tight
like an old wooden window sash
on a chalk-pink house,
front yard roses,
voluptuous heads, overripe,
springing incongruously
from bare dirt on barbed rods.
That's me with my bleached hair,
barefoot on the porch,
smoking and waiting.
Apparently I'll meet you there
time and time again.

Valerian

When she was depressed
she drank valerian tea.
She bought the chopped up dried root
at the health food store
and kept little bags of it lying around.
It smelled horrible, like dirty socks.
Funny thing, too, is how
she used to hate the valerian
that grew wild all over
the back yard where she
and her husband used to live,
with the neat little beds of roses,
and all around them stood
the valerian, wild and tall
with roots so strong
they could break up a patio.
In the end she gave up
trying to get rid of them
and decided it was nature's plan
for patios,
that they would break up anyway
like sheets of ice
and drift slowly apart.

Wine Coolers

Think of your life,
I begin, sipping a wine cooler,
As a herd of wildebeest, and your husband
as the weakest link in the herd,
and Jodi, the lioness, that must
by nature's law, bring down
that weakest link...No.

Think of your husband
as something thick and sticky
like rubber cement
and Jodi is pulling him off you, freeing you...No.
He's something dry, brittle and ossified
and she's a jackhammer, breaking him up,
and I just want to float away
on a piece of broken patio...
I pour myself another wine cooler,

Think of Jodi as a fly, I begin again,
You live for years with your husband
drinking wine coolers that you don't even like
when all along she's in the house,
checking out wallpaper,
measuring windows
and just circling.

Offering

She takes a pie out of the oven
and holds it before her.
Her family is gathered around her,
yet she moves like a woman alone
in a golden field, barefoot,
scanning for a high spot,
a large outcropping, on which to place
the offering, perhaps a large rock,
someplace that a mountain
or sky god would be sure to see it.
She would cry out his name,
but it has no vowels.
It has no consonants, either
just the thrill of offering
as she places the pie
on the table.

Wisdom of Hands

Entering again through the stone gate,
where once soft hands fluttered,
holding drinks, electric mixers,
salad bowls prepared for guests,
combining and recombining
the elements of offering
according to the laws of creation.
Now leathery hands grind roots and bark,
bones and berries.
In silence and solitude
an old woman brews a cup of tea
in the chill light of dawn.

Journey

Girl dived down to the bottom of a river
and felt with her two hands
the rough brick and the chipped paint
of a porch.
Her angel told her not to be afraid
but to be like a golden fish swimming freely
through the waters of life.
So she enjoyed the persimmons
and calendula and valerian,
the figs and the fruit of the prickly pear
but mostly she enjoyed the children,
that she had fed loquats and pomegranates,
tiny peaches and plums, cakes and bread,
and while the old house was falling
down around them
she painted the refrigerator midnight blue,
hung a whale poster over the tub
and washed the dishes, handpainted with koi,
arms deep in the waters of life.

The Gifts

There I am, twelve years old,
soaking my yellow dress as I drink
from the stone fountain,
frogs all around,
my hands, impossibly graceful
in sheer, fitted gloves
whose seams halo my fingers
like a fairy godmother's gift.

A wrinkled hand sifts and scoops
from sacks of roots and leaves,
combining, weighing. Take.
This is the formula. It takes you back,
again and again, until all is salvaged.

The old porch is weathered
and chipped, a ship run aground.
A child holds out her hand
to show the woman a stone.
The woman doesn't look,
she is scanning the horizon
in jeans and flipflops,
one hand shading her brow.

Wedgewood Stove

There's a bottle of wine on the table
and a glass in my hand,
I open the book,
there's always a book,
there's always a whale poster,
over a clawfoot tub,
there's always Nina Simone on the stereo,
and a floor heater to dance around,
there's always bamboo by the shed
for the kids to jump into from the roof,
there's always a wedgewood stove,
a pile of laundry,
a pot of beans,
there's always a cracked patio
out the kitchen door,
and when you stood there looking up,
a cigarette in your hand,
there was always a hole in the sky
with light raining down.

Lifeline

Over and over, I wander these rocky bluffs,
sometimes there is a window
through the clouds.
One clear day I spot a ladder,
an old woman welcomes me.
A party is in full swing.
Paisley shirts, Luther Vandross,
cigar-smoking bikers,
a girl in yellow chiffon.
Staring into a wine cooler
I contemplate the mysteries,
here is how wisdom dawns:
like a lilac sunset,
a wrinkled hand,
a tendril curling on a vine,
a mortar and pestle, grinding.

Sparks

The day my kids started
the old shed on fire
flames floating over faded wallpaper
revealing layer after layer
Chinese writing, linoleum patches
smiling faces on old newspapers
curling off in the smoke.
We were able to put it out
with a hose and drag
out an old mattress
to lie on the cement, those old
mattresses could go on
burning for days
the fire burrowing deep
inside the thick cotton
impossible to quench.
For days it rained softly
we watched thin streams of smoke
rise through bare wet branches
while deep inside all that soaked cotton
sparks still smoldered, alive
inside nests of fire
waiting to burst out
like so many red bees.

Diamond Pattern

A faded diamond pattern appears
an old linoleum floor
in the heart of the house.
I can almost see my chipped toenail polish
and the french wallpaper
partly hidden by the long stringy strands
of a mop draped down over it.
Memory Hag!
A mop dragged back and forth,
washing, scrubbing, erasing things
I want to remember
the frosting smudge,
the birthday cake crumbs,
but leaving the really tough stains,
here, where I was drunk and swerved
all the way to my car
and there, where I scraped out a living
like scraping kernels
from an ear of corn
with my bare hands.

Vintage

The old house resonates with the presence
of the Italians who lived there before...
They are the old men, sipping wine.
They are the ones who buried the shoes
and nailed cans full of bolts
and screws to the shed wall,
and left jars of canned plums in the basement...
they are the ones who planted walnut,
almond, plum, pomegranate,
persimmon, peach, and yes, prickly pear
they called tuna cactus,
for the stickery fruit.
They sit there still on the cracked patio,
tasting of the new wine...they nod,
knowing it will age and be transformed
but it will take time, time. Be patient, girl.
The pissed off single mother stands
on the porch, hands on her hips.
The old house isn't much
but she likes the fruit trees
and the cutting board,
extra long, for making ravioli.

Prickly Pear

She knew now that what she needed
was all this pale sand,
so cleansing and elemental, gently abrasive.
She set down the small paper bag
containing the prickly pear, wondering how
anyone ever got at the sweet fruit.
Wondering that anyone tried.
The old man next door had handed her the brown bag,
saying, "So delicious.
You just have to be careful. Use a pliers."
Maybe she should just dig a deep hole
and drop it in.
Then no one would get hurt.
But infinite as the sand appears
the tides have the power to sweep back
vast curtains of it, and there it would be;
A dangerous fruit bleeding into the sand,
thorns threatening furiously.
No. She'd keep it.
She had a pliers.
And she had to taste it.

Logos

The girl cannot see that the woman
in jeans and flipflops
is the woman she will become,
hands pulling out
the extra long cutting board,
making ravioli, putting up wallpaper.
The woman cannot see the laughing child
looking down from the ceiling,
the hand reaching down,
moving things about
as in a dollhouse.

Reaching down in the garden,
parting huge primeval leaves to peer
at the one big green pumpkin,
the woman knows that just as in Genesis
all things are created by a flaming word,
so there is a logos of change,
turning green pumpkins orange,
--oh not all at once like the Rapture--
but there all along,
a candle, flickering in the background,
angels in the Torah bending over
each blade of grass, whispering
Grow!

Janet Trenchard is an artist and writer. Her paintings and assemblages have been exhibited in San Jose, Palo Alto, Carmel and San Francisco. She has had poems and stories (some published under the name Janet Crawford) in Porter Gulch Review, Paisley Moon, Hilltromper, Caesura, and other journals.

You can find her paintings on-line: http://janettrenchardart.weebly.com and her poems at: www.bluebonebooks.com

This book may or may not have been channeled through a couple of old Italian men sitting on a patio.

www.ingramcontent.com/pod-product-compliance
Lightning Source LLC
Chambersburg PA
CBHW050605300426
44112CB00013B/2089